CHRISTMAS IS...

Devotions for the Season

adapted from past Christmas-season sermons
given by
Pastor Bryan Koch
Glad Tidings Assembly of God

Morning Joy Media

Spring City, Pennsylvania

Published by Morning Joy Media.

Visit www.morningjoymedia.com for more information on bulk discounts and special promotions, or e-mail your questions to info@morningjoymedia.com.

Unless otherwise noted, Scripture quotations are taken from the Holy Bible, New International Version®, NIV®. Copyright © 1973, 1978, 1984 by Biblica, Inc.™ Used by permission of Zondervan. All rights reserved worldwide.

Design: Staci Focht

Cataloging-In-Publication Data

Subject Headings:
   1. Christmas—Prayers and devotions. 2. Advent—Prayers and devotions. 3. Christian life. I. Title.

ISBN 978-1-937107-13-0

Printed in the United States of America

Table of Contents

This book is dedicated to the Lord Jesus Christ, Who is Christmas.

"But when the time had fully come, God sent his Son, born of a woman, born under the law..." (Galatians 4:4)

Introduction

*C*hristmas is ...

That's a blank I've been attempting to fill in for many years now. At the very foundation Christmas is a story, a truly amazing story. One could easily argue it is the central story that the entire Word of God points to. In Genesis 3:15 we read,

> *"And I will put enmity between you and the woman, and between your offspring and hers; he will crush your head, and you will strike his heel."*

This prophetic word is spoken by God the Father about Jesus Christ to the enemy of mankind.

I suppose that every year when December rolls around, we all find ourselves thinking about what Christmas is. I guess the danger of well-known stories, even miraculous ones, is that they can become familiar to the point that we stop even trying to fill in the blank.

My heart for each of you is that *Christmas Is...* will help prepare you once again for this season. My prayer for each of you is that this devotional created from Christmas Eves gone by will stir you again with memories, wonder, reflection, and the meaning of all that Christmas is and can be. In the words of the Apostle Peter,

> "So I will always remind you of these things, even though you know them and are firmly established in the truth you now have. I think it is right to refresh your memory as long as I live in the tent of this body." (2 Peter 1:12–13).

Christmas is...all about Jesus.

Bryan

CHRISTMAS IS...

Light

The Collision

The people walking in darkness have seen a great light; on those living in the land of the shadow of death a light has dawned. (Isaiah 9:2)

For to us a child is born, to us a son is given, and the government will be on his shoulders. And he will be called Wonderful Counselor, Mighty God, Everlasting Father, Prince of Peace. (Isaiah 9:6)

The 400 years between the Old and New Testaments was a very dark period of time for God's people. Although God had stopped talking to the Jews, Isaiah's prophesy radiated the truth that God would continue to provide for His chosen people. Just like God delivered the Jews out of the bondage of Egypt, He would bring hope and light even during the dark period of Roman occupation of the land promised to the descendants of Abraham, Isaac, and Jacob. It was against this backdrop of darkness and despair that Jesus was born. Many times we see Christmas as shopping for gifts, preparing the perfect menu, wishing for snow in the forecast, but rarely do we see Christmas as a collision. In truth, Christmas is a collision between heaven and earth. It is when God's love collides with our needs.

★ In what areas of your life is there a need for a collision of God's love?

....

....

....

....

★ From what bondages has God delivered you?

....

....

....

....

....

Illumination

And there were shepherds living out in the fields nearby, keeping watch over their flocks at night. An angel of the Lord appeared to them, and the glory of the Lord shone around them, and they were terrified. But the angel said to them, "Do not be afraid. I bring you good news of great joy that will be for all people." (Luke 2:8—10)

The shepherds are some of my favorite people in the Bible. They are the third-shift guys in a society that held the profession of a shepherd in low esteem. They didn't get to enjoy the amenities of life that most people had in the villages and the cities, but God chose to first share the good news with the least among us and He did it at night. The angel of the Lord illuminated a dark sky while sharing the good news with the shepherds.

Once the angel returned to heaven,

...the shepherds said to one another, "Let's go to Bethlehem and see this thing that has happened, which the Lord has told us about." (Luke 2:-15)

and they left the field in search of the light of the world, a baby in a manger.

★ When God's light illuminates your darkness, what will your journey to Bethlehem look like?

★ How can you share the good news to people living in darkness?

Reflection

For you were once darkness, but now you are light in the Lord. Live as children of light. (Ephesians 5:8)

For he has rescued us from the dominion of darkness and brought us into the kingdom of the Son he loves. (Colossians 1:13)

Have you ever seen kids playing with a laser pointer? The fun in using a laser pointer is that we can't trace the source of the light. The beam of light cannot be seen until it reflects off of an object. Actually, all light can only be seen when it is reflected off of something else. When we see the reflection of light, we also need to believe that there is a direct connection with the source of that light. Just like no man has seen the actual source of light, no man has seen God, but we do see God in others; God's light reflects off of us and our lives. We are the reflection of God's purposes. God wants us to be a light in the world, and Christ is the only way to personal illumination.

★ In what ways have you been a reflection of light for God?

★ What opportunities have you missed to be a reflection of light to others?

★ How can you be more mindful in your daily life to be a reflection of God's light?

Darkness

*Darkness comes upon them in the daytime;
at noon they grope as in the night. (Job 5:14)*

One of my jobs in the Koch household is to turn off the outdoor Christmas lights, which I usually do in bare feet running as quickly as I can back into my house. Transitioning inside where all of the lights are off, I start to get used to the dark. Sure I might stumble through rooms or look up the stairs with uncertainty, but I adjust. Our lives are like this, too; we can get used to the dark. Walking through life without God's light will create the same feelings of stumbling and uncertainty. Add to that, fear. When we ask the Holy Spirit to show us the dark spots in our lives, we begin the process of shedding light on those areas. Maybe it's being ruled by emotions, addiction, or sin; but whatever it is, when the light of Christ penetrates that darkness, it will hurt at first and then the healing begins. In this process, repent in these areas and turn them over to God.

As those dark spots are illuminated and you begin radiating light in all areas, just think how much sunscreen the devil will have to wear around you!

★ What are the dark areas of your life that Christ's light needs to penetrate and heal?

....

....

....

....

....

★ Why does it sometimes seem to be easier to remain in the dark?

....

....

....

....

....

....

Christmas Prayer 2010

When Jesus spoke again to the people, he said, "I am the light of the world. Whoever follows me will never walk in darkness, but will have the light of life." (John 8:-12)

Father, thank You for Your glorious light that has shined in our lives and Lord, as we respond to that light may we not get caught up in the aesthetics of this season, but really understand it's all about You, about a relationship with You, about the light You bring into our lives. Invade all of the places of our heart, our unbelief, all of the things we've kept to ourselves. Receive the greatest gift that can ever be received. Salvation. The forgiveness of sins. Lord, we confess with our mouth and we believe in our heart that You are God's Son. We ask God that You have Your way in spirit and in truth. Amen.

CHRISTMAS IS...

Peace

Peace of God

For to us a child is born, to us a son is given, and the government will be on his shoulders. And he will be called Wonderful Counselor, Mighty God, Everlasting Father, Prince of Peace. (Isaiah 9:6)

Although Isaiah gave Jesus several names, the last name he prophesied is Prince of Peace. When we look around, how many of us really sense peace at Christmas? A Sunday school teacher asked her class, "What is Christmas?" She got the usual answers like a birthday celebration, joy, and worship, but one boy responded, "Christmas is about good sportsmanship because we don't ever get what we want." When I was younger, my sister and I begged our parents to let us open just one gift on Christmas Eve. It was after midnight, so technically it was Christmas. Our parents made us wait and I remember running into the living room in the morning and seeing a really small box and a really big box. Well, my sister got an organ for Christmas that year, and I got a watch. I didn't want an organ, but it was such a big gift that I wished it had been mine. The truth is that no person can give us what we truly want and need. Wouldn't it be awesome, though, if we could wrap up the peace of God and hand it to someone? The good news is that the gift of peace is available to us at all times. God wrapped up peace and He gave it to us. He didn't wrap it up in a box and bow; He wrapped it in flesh. He wrapped it up with His Son and He offered it to us.

★ What gifts do you most value?

....

....

....

★ How will you use God's gift of peace this year?

....

....

....

Peace with God

And through him to reconcile to himself all things, whether things on earth or things in heaven, by making peace through his blood, shed on the cross. Once you were alienated from God and were enemies in your minds because of your evil behavior. But now he has reconciled you by Christ's physical body through death to present you holy in his sight, without blemish and free from accusation. (Colossians 1:20–22)

*T*his is not often Scripture that we hear at Christmas, but there is no peace *of* God until we have peace *with* God.

Therefore, since we have been justified through faith, we have peace with God through our Lord Jesus Christ. (Romans 5:1)

We make peace with God through belief in Jesus Christ. Until that occurs we may have fleeting moments of peace, but we'll never have the peace that surpasses all understanding. If I haven't made my peace with God, then underneath the external happiness will be that nagging war that rages between God and me. When we put our complete faith and trust in Jesus Christ, our salvation is settled and we have peace with God.

★ How do you know when you have peace with God?

....

....

....

....

....

★ Describe your sense of peace.

....

....

....

....

....

Peace with Myself

The mind of sinful man is death, but the mind controlled by the Spirit is life and peace. (Romans 8:6)

Carnality produces unrest in our lives. When we claim to follow Christ and still chase after fleshly desires, we will not have peace. Living in two worlds produces turmoil. When we make right choices and pursue the spiritual things of God, the peace of God results. Being spiritually minded produces peace.

Let the peace of Christ rule in your hearts, since as members of one body you were called to peace. And be thankful (Colossians 3:-15)

Fighting God for control of our lives creates a lack of peace. For some strange reason we think we can handle life better than He can. When we try to control our situation rather than simply understanding that He is in control, we rob ourselves of peace. Friends, we don't know anything about our lives more than what God knows.

★ How can you live in the world, but still have a heart and mind controlled by the Spirit?

....

....

....

....

....

....

★ How have you tried to handle life on your own? What was the result?

....

....

....

....

....

Peace with Others

If it is possible, as far as it depends on you, live at peace with everyone. (Romans 12:18)

"I have told you these things, so that in me you may have peace. In this world you will have trouble. But take heart! I have overcome the world." (John 16:33)

Advent either magnifies our joy or our pain. If you're headed for divorce, if you've lost a loved one, or if you've experienced relational riffs, this season intensifies that pain and hampers the peace of God. There are wars both large and small going on in the world today. News of human brutality fills the airwaves each night. If our definition of peace is the absence of conflict, then we will not experience the peace that God has provided for us. Jesus came into the world among turmoil and He ascended from this earth under the most brutal circumstances, but Christ's promise was one of peace.

"Peace I leave with you; my peace I give you. I do not give to you as the world gives. Do not let your hearts be troubled and do not be afraid." (John 14:27)

In the midst of human strife God will give us peace.

★ When you experience conflict in your life, how can you rely on God's peace to get you through the difficult times?

....

....

....

....

★ How can you have peace with others?

....

....

....

....

....

Christmas Prayer 2009

"Glory to God in the highest, and on earth peace to men on whom his favor rests." Luke 2:-14)

Dear Father, there is nothing we want or need more than a relationship with You. We are celebrating Your gift to the world wrapped in flesh. Thank You Lord for the peace You have given us. The peace of our Savior Jesus Christ. God, as we light candles this Christmas season, may we remember all Your gifts to us and all that You have done for us. And God, when we extinguish those candles, we ask Lord that it not be an ending, but a beginning. A beginning of the freedom from pain and hurt. The beginning of peace in our lives. Amen.

CHRISTMAS IS...

The Power of One

The Power of One

"Now this is eternal life: that they may know you, the only true God, and Jesus Christ, whom you have sent." (John 17:3)

"I will remain in the world no longer, but they are still in the world, and I am coming to you Holy Father, protect them by the power of your name—the name you gave me—so that they may be one as we are one." (John 17:11)

Rarely do we think of *one* as powerful. If someone asked, "How many people are on the team?" or "How many people listened to the service?" and the answer was "one," we might raise an eyebrow thinking that one certainly doesn't sound very impressive. Sometimes, though, one can be very powerful. One degree can take a wet road and make it an icy road. One degree can take hot water and make it boiling water. Think about the power of one word, one thought, one decision. One decision this Christmas Eve, a one degree change, can cause you to soar instead of flat-lining and living the same old life.

★ What one degree change can you make to soar and have the life that God intends for you?

....

....

....

★ Words have power both for good and for evil. What words build up and what words tear down?

....

....

★ How can you be more conscious of the words you use on a daily basis?

....

....

★ With whom do you need to be more gentle in your approach?

....

....

It's Okay to Cry

In those days Caesar Augustus issued a decree that a census should be taken of the entire Roman world. (This was the first census that took place while Quirinius was governor of Syria.) And everyone went to his own town to register. So Joseph also went up from the town of Nazareth in Galilee to Judea, to Bethlehem the town of David, because he belonged to the house and line of David. He went there to register with Mary, who was pledged to be married to him and was expecting a child. While they were there, the time came for the baby to be born, and she gave birth to her firstborn, a son. She wrapped him in cloths and placed him in a manger, because there was no room for them in the inn. (Luke 2:1-7)

Christmas is one day out of 365 days. When Christmas comes, life doesn't go on hold; problems don't stop, people die, hurt still happens. Sometimes we cry at Christmas, not for the joy or gratitude of what God has done, but for the pain we feel. I just want to say to you that it's okay to cry because tears during this holy season are consistent with what really happened the first Christmas. It wasn't all the gold and the glitz and the shopping and the rushing. It wasn't all clean and sterile and perfect. There were problems the first Christmas. There were economic problems: Caesar Augustus issued a decree for everyone to return to their homes to prepare for a heavy tax. There was inconvenience: Mary was pregnant and had to travel not by bus or train or plane, but by a donkey. There was violence: Herod ordered the killing of all males under the age of two. Friends, the first Christmas was by no means sterile and by no means perfect. If this year your life isn't on hold, if this Christmas has magnified your pain, it's okay to cry.

★ How can remembering the problems that Joseph and Mary faced the first Christmas

help you deal with your own pain and heart-
ache this season and throughout the year?

One Life

For if, by the trespass of the one man, death reigned through that one man, how much more will those who receive God's abundant provision of grace and of the gift of righteousness reign in life through the one man, Jesus Christ. Consequently, just as the result of one trespass was condemnation for all men, so also the result of one act of righteousness was justification that brings life for all men. For just as through the disobedience of the one man the many were made sinners, so also through the obedience of the one man the many will be made righteous. (Romans 5:17–19)

One life brought sin into the world, and one life saved it. Life has the power for good and for evil. Think about your life. How powerful is it? Consider our average day: we sleep, get up, eat, get dressed, go to work, watch TV, spend some time on our hobbies and then repeat the whole process over again. Doesn't sound very powerful, does it? Our lives become valuable when we connect our life with God's life. When we reach out to God and establish a relationship with Him because He's already reached out to us, that's when our lives become powerful. Life is a gift that has been given to each of us. As we go through our day connected to God, He will guide us on our journey. We will impact the people we meet and do the work God wants us to do to further His kingdom. That's a powerful life.

★ In what ways do you feel your life has become routine?

....

....

....

★ What people in your life have had a positive impact on you?

....

....

....

★ What did they say and what did they do?

★ Consider the people that God has put in your path. What positive impact did you or can you have on them?

One Man

Then Peter began to speak: "I now realize
how true it is that God does not show
favoritism but accepts men from every
nation who fear him and do what is right.
You know the message God sent to the people
of Israel, telling the good news of peace
through Jesus Christ, who is Lord of all. You
know what has happened throughout Judea,
beginning in Galilee after the baptism that
John preached—how God anointed Jesus of
Nazareth with the Holy Spirit and power,
and how he went around doing good and
healing all who were under the power of the
devil, because God was with him.
(Acts 10:34–38)

Jesus. He never traveled more than 200
miles from His home. His friends de-
serted Him. He was turned over to His enemies
and nailed to a cross to hang between two thieves.
When He died, He was laid in a borrowed grave.
By modern standards this isn't the kind of resumé

that defines success; however, two thousand years ago, the baby in the manger, whose hands were so small they could barely grasp Mary's finger, those are the hands that created the world. Today, Jesus is the centerpiece of life. He is our Cornerstone, Healer, Redeemer, Morning Star, and Savior. He has transformed the world and us. And friends, Jesus Christ is coming back not as a frail baby but as the King of Kings and Lord of Lords. He is coming back with power. There is no other name and no other way. There is no self-help book, no pulling ourselves up by our boot straps. We are in a sinful world and the only way out of the muck and the mire is to embrace the one and only Son of God.

So it is written: The first man Adam became a living being"; the last Adam, a life-giving spirit. (1 Corinthians 15:45)

★ How do you define success?

★ What does your spiritual resumé look like?

....

....

....

....

....

★ After reviewing Jesus' resumé, how would you redefine success?

....

....

....

....

....

....

....

....

Christmas Prayer 2008

"How will this be," Mary asked the angel, "since I am a virgin?" The angel answered, "The Holy Spirit will come upon you, and the power of the Most High will overshadow you. So the holy one to be born will be called the Son of God. Even Elizabeth your relative is going to have a child in her old age, and she who was said to be barren is in her sixth month. For nothing is impossible with God."
(Luke 1:34–37)

Father, we thank You for Your incredible love and power. Thank You for the price You paid. Thank You that You weren't just born and You didn't just come to us; but You lived, You healed, You died for our sins, and You rose again on the third day and ascended back into heaven and even now You sit at His right hand. God, thank You that You are honored by the transparency of those who need to connect with You. Lord, I pray that today You would touch hearts and Your Word says that if we will confess Jesus' name, all our sins are forgiven, that we would be saved not by our works but by Your gift. Jesus, that's our goal today that each one of us would move one step closer to You, that our one life would connect with Your one powerful solitary life. God, You know our hearts and I pray that You have begun a powerful work in them, for with You nothing is impossible. Amen.

CHRISTMAS IS...

A Shake Up

The Blueprint

But when the time had fully come, God sent his Son, born of a woman, born under law, to redeem those under law, that we might receive the full rights of sons. (Galatians 4:4–5)

The birth of Jesus shook up the world, but how did He arrive on earth at just the right time? God spent 4,000 years planning for the birth of His Son. God used the Jews during that time to spread the word that there was only one God, Jehovah. The Greeks and Romans had many gods, and at the time of Jesus' birth the world was a pagan world, so the time was right spiritually. There were 400 years of silence between the Old and New Testaments. There were no prophets, no Scripture was written; Heaven seemed silent. The years that the Jews spent proclaiming that the Messiah would come to save the world from their sins came to fruition when Jesus was born. The Roman Empire was linguistically divided with one half speaking Latin and the other half speaking

Greek. It took some time, but eventually Greek was adopted by the empire as the universal language; the time was right culturally. Having one language allowed the disciples to take the message of Jesus to the whole world. Because Rome controlled the world, the time was right politically. Having one government and a highly organized road system allowed the disciples to travel safely from place to place to spread the word of Jesus. When we begin to ponder God's timing of the birth of Christ, we need to realize that the truth is when Jesus was born the blueprint had already been drawn.

★ What plans have you spent a lot of time making that didn't turn out as you expected?

★ When you look back at those times, in what ways do you see God's plan for your life working instead?

Priorities

Because you are sons, God sent the Spirit of his Son into our hearts, the Spirit who calls out, "Abba, Father." So you are no longer a slave, but a son; and since you are a son, God has made you also an heir. (Galatians 4:6–7)

God wants to shake up our priorities. When we allow God into our lives, He changes our direction, desires, and destiny. When we make God the director of our lives, we no longer chase after sin but pursue righteousness following Christ and His plan. God wants to be in our lives and although we may struggle with sinful desires, our ultimate desire is to live worthy of our Lord. We begin to pray, read the Bible, and seek a relationship with Him. When Christ enters our lives, He doesn't erase the past, but He changes how we relate to it, giving us perspective of how to live in the present. God changes our hopes and goals for the future, therefore changing our destiny.

★ What are your priorities for this coming year?

....

....

....

....

....

★ What events from your past can you now put
in perspective and use for good in the present?

....

....

....

....

....

....

....

....

The Miracle of the Moment

And Mary said: "My soul glorifies the Lord and my spirit rejoices in God my Savior, for he has been mindful of the humble state of his servant. From now on all generations will call me blessed, for the Mighty One has done great things for me— holy is his name. (Luke 1:46–49)

*H*ow many times do we miss the miracle of the moment because all around us seems to be chaos? How many times has something small happened that we brushed off as insignificant only to learn later that it was a big deal after all? How many times have we felt annoyed or worried about something only to realize the blessing that was really there? Think of the events that transpired the first Christmas and the miracle of the moment. Think of Mary; she gets a visit from the angel Gabriel who says to her,

"Greetings, you who are highly favored! The Lord is with you". (Luke 1:28)

The next verse reveals that Mary was greatly troubled by this greeting and at the time did not feel highly favored. Now, think about Joseph; he's in a tough spot being engaged to a woman who's pregnant and Joseph knows he isn't the father. What will the neighbors say? How will their relatives react? He doesn't want to disgrace Mary, but he also doesn't want to be in this situation either. Once Mary and Joseph learn that God has entrusted them with His Son, Jesus Christ, their fears and worries melt away and they embrace the miracle of the moment.

★ In what relationships do you need to be less judgmental and more supportive?

★ What needs to be rearranged or refocused in your life so that you notice and embrace the miracles of the moment?

The Nativity

Through him all things were made; without him nothing was made that has been made. (John 1:3)

He was in the world, and though the world was made through him, the world did not recognize him. He came to that which was his own, but his own did not receive him. Yet to all who received him, to those who believed in his name, he gave the right to become children of God (John 1:10—12)

*E*very year the number of Nativity scenes set up in both private and public spaces gets fewer and fewer. There are even some places that will put up a Nativity but will leave out the Baby Jesus. In more and more areas of life Jesus is being left out. He has been taken out of our schools and our government. Jesus has even been taken out of Christmas, replaced instead with a man in a red suit carrying a sack stuffed with gifts that will one day very likely end up in a landfill. Friends, without Christ we don't have Christmas, and without Christ we don't have hope. The biblical definition of hope is the expectation of a favorable future under the direction of God. When we take Christ out of Christmas, we take hope out of our lives. The birth of Jesus shook the world, but remember a snow globe doesn't come to life until it's shaken, and we won't come to life until we accept Jesus as our Lord and Savior. Allow God to shake up your Christmas. Keep Him at the center of all you do. Keep Christ in Christmas.

★ What are some traditions that you have in your family that are most meaningful to you?

★ If Jesus isn't the center of Christmas for you, what has replaced Him? How can you put Christ back in Christmas?

Christmas Prayer 2007

Many, O Lord my God, are the wonders you have done. The things you planned for us no one can recount to you; were I to speak and tell of them, they would be too many to declare. (Psalm 40:5)

Thank You, Father for Your love. Thank You God for the first day You shook our life. Lord, we admit to You that sometimes we are so focused on and anxious about the future that we forget the past and what You have done and we forget the moment we live in. I pray that You would help us to realize the miracle of this moment. You shook the world, You want to speak to us, You want us to understand what this Christmas celebration is really about. We open our hearts and ask You to help us in this time as we hear the truth of Your Word. Help us embrace everything You want to speak to us so that it can change our lives. We pray for Your blessing that there will be an expectation of a favorable future for every person. We love You, Lord. May Your love and light reflect in our lives. Amen.

CHRISTMAS IS...

A Gift

The Receiver

On coming to the house, they saw the child
with his mother Mary, and they bowed down
and worshiped him. Then they opened
their treasures and presented him with
gifts of gold and of incense and of myrrh.
(Matthew 2:11)

*G*ifts convey a message; a gift says as much
about the person giving it as it does
about the person receiving it. When the Magi
journeyed to Bethlehem, they bought gifts for the
baby Jesus. The gifts were by no means practical;
they were prophetic. Think about when Jesus
came into this world the humble beginning He
had lying in a manger inside of a stable and then
contrast that with the gift of gold. Why did the
Magi give Jesus gold? Through this gift the Magi
recognized that before them was the one true King.
Because the smoke from frankincense rises, this
gift symbolized Jesus as our Mediator. Even before
the baby Jesus could talk, the Magi saw Him as our

Intercessor. In biblical times myrrh was used in such funeral preparations as anointing the dead. It's an odd gift to give a baby, but not to the One who would become the Savior of mankind. When the Magi gave myrrh to baby Jesus, it symbolized His death and prophesied that Jesus came to the world to die for the world. Gold. Frankincense. Myrrh. Prophetic gifts given the first Christmas. Jesus Christ is our King, our Mediator, and our Savior.

★ In what ways will focusing on the meaning of the gifts given to Jesus the first Christmas alter your perceptions, attitudes, and thoughts this holiday season?

★ What gifts do you have that you can use to be a blessing to the Lord?

The Right Gift

"For God so loved the world that he gave his one and only Son, that whoever believes in him shall not perish but have eternal life." (John 3:-16)

Cost, need, and motivation all determine the rightness of a gift. When I was four years old, I received the right gift for Christmas, a Lone Ranger costume. I don't know what it cost, but it was as close to authentic as a four-year-old could possibly want—complete with mask, white hat, boots, and matching holster. The need it met fulfilled my inner cowboy. My parents knew I loved the Lone Ranger, so their motivation was to give me a gift that would make me very happy, and it did. It's one of my favorite gifts from my childhood, but as the years pressed on, I outgrew the costume. Every gift we give will not last forever, but the gifts God gives to His people, they last forever. God gave the world the greatest gift when He sent us His Son, Jesus Christ. God gave us not only the right gift, but the perfect gift. When we consider the cost, there couldn't be a more perfect gift. There is nothing that the Father could have given us that could have cost more; Jesus Christ is the treasure of heaven. When it comes to need—to the right gift—what could fill the needs of men more than our Savior? What could help us in our spiritual longing, our sin, and our sense of being lost? Finally, God loved us before we ever loved Him. God's motives are completely pure, and His love for us is pure. God didn't run out at the last minute for a gift for mankind. Remember, God gave His Son.

★ What was one of the best Christmas gifts you ever received?

★ How will you look at gift-giving differently this Christmas?

The Gift of Restoration

But Esau ran to meet Jacob and embraced him; he threw his arms around his neck and kissed him. And they wept. (Genesis 33:4)

..."If I have found favor in your eyes, accept this gift from me. For to see your face is like seeing the face of God, now that you have received me favorably. Please accept the present that was brought to you, for God has been gracious to me and I have all I need." And because Jacob insisted, Esau accepted it. (Genesis 33:10—11)

Gifts can strengthen relationships and heal broken ones. Jacob had a great deal to make up for after pilfering Esau's blessing and inheritance by deceiving their father, Isaac. Jacob mends his relationship with his brother Esau by sending gifts. Greater than the gifts that Jacob presents to his brother is Esau's gift of forgiveness of Jacob.

Bear with each other and forgive whatever grievances you may have against one another. Forgive as the Lord forgave you. (Colossians 3:-13)

The gift that God gives to us in His Son is a relationship builder. When we receive the gift of salvation from God, He restores the brokenness in us, between us, and with Him. We no longer live a life separate from God but one in relationship to Him.

★ What relationships in your life could use the gift of forgiveness?

★ What steps can you take to help restore that relationship?

★ In what ways can you strengthen your relationship with God?

The Unopened Gift

*And this is the testimony: God has given
us eternal life, and this life is in his Son.
He who has the Son has life; he who does not
have the Son of God does not have life.
(1 John 5:11–12)*

During the 2006 Christmas season the
congregation answered the question,
"What was your life before Christ and after
accepting Christ?" I spent a few hours one after-
noon reading the responses and was touched by
what people said they received from God after
accepting Jesus as their Lord and Savior: Love,
Freedom, Peace, Joy, Perspective, Forgiveness,
Healing, Purpose, and Eternal Life. I walked away
from my office that day and I thought, "Those are
the real gifts; the gifts that can't be wrapped up."
I felt the greatness of God as I left the church that
day, but I also felt a sense of sadness. The Father
has done so much for us and has provided for us
more than we could ever hope for on our own that

it puzzles me people still don't receive His gift. There's nothing we can do to earn this gift. We can't work hard enough for it; we can't be good enough to get it. All we have to do is receive it, but for many people God's gift remains the unopened gift, that one gift left under the tree to sit by itself day after day waiting to be opened. When we do finally extend our arms and receive God's gift, all the real gifts in life are ours and as joy unspeakable fills our spirit, we can only express our gratitude; as Paul proclaimed,

Thanks be to God for his indescribable gift!"
(2 Corinthians 9:-15)

★ What is still unopened under your tree?

....

....

....

....

....

....

★ Why have you left these gifts unopened?

Christmas Prayer 2006

For the wages of sin is death, but the gift of God is eternal life in Christ Jesus our Lord. (Romans 6:23)

Dear Father, we thank You that You have given us the greatest gift, the most fitting gift, the right gift that every one of us needs. We pray that as a result of Your gift, this Christmas lives will be changed. To the one who is drifting from You, the one who is in a broken relationship, the one who is disheartened, the one who is lonely, the one who needs healing—Lord, we ask You for Your gift of restoration as only You can give in Your Son, Jesus Christ. Lord, we pray that like the Magi who worshiped and went home a different way that today we may go home a different way full of hope, joy, peace, love, and the promise of eternal life. Lord, help those who are still lost to stretch out their hands to You and open Your precious gift. Help all of us make You the center of our lives, God. We thank You, Father, for all You have done for us and for Your indescribable gift. Amen.

Additional Resources

The devotions and prayers from *Christmas Is...* have been adapted from past Glad Tidings Christmas sermons. The following sermon series are available for purchase in Scrolls Bookstore:

★ **Adventageous**: In this series, we explore Advent and discover why Jesus coming to earth is ADVENTageous for all of us.

★ **Illuminate**: Through this series, you will learn how the fulfillment of prophecies about Christ's birth "illuminates" the inspiration of God's Word.

★ **The Power of One:** This series shows us that there is great power in just taking that one step to draw closer to God.

★ **Shake Up Your Christmas:** This series brings to light that God wants to shake up our priorities and have Christmas come alive in our hearts.